Pam,

I hope you enjoy the story and message from my book. Thank you for always seeing the value in Mike. I adore you for that. God's favor and blessings on you always!

Warmest regards,

Deb C

Stepping Stones

Creating Personal Integrity

DEBBIE GREER CHAMBERLAIN

Print ISBN: 978-1-66780-144-5
eBook ISBN: 978-1-66780-145-2

Table of Contents

Stepping Stones:

CREATING PERSONAL INTEGRITY

Stepping stones through life … because a life's journey is never a straight line. The choices we make in life are steps that take downward, upward, and sideway motion. We can make choices that may alter our journey from our intended path. We all have a path or calling that will tug at our hearts and soul until we find our purpose and work that we were placed here to do. The challenge is to find a way to make these "steps" or choices count so the direction leads us on a path of joy, peace, happiness, and fulfillment. The problem for most people while navigating their life lies in the constant change of direction. The past, the present, and even the thought of the future can get in our way. Our past can also play a major role in our choices about life. Our thoughts and the choices we make determine our ability to move on in becoming who we were meant to be. I believe that the choices you make, whether they were made with good intention or no thought at all can leave you in a misery of your own making or a life filled with promise and joy.

I know how hard it is to live a life that is fulfilling and one where you feel you have found your purpose. I had faced more challenges from life before I was seven years old than most people face in a lifetime. As a young child who was abused and then abandoned, I grew up in a group Children's

Home and was raised by a religious based organization. At the age of eleven, I went to live at the Children's Home after being abused and abandoned twice. I was first left by my mother at the age of seven and then again by my father at the age eleven. Being placed in the Children's Home by my grandparents was the turning point of my life. This event was one of the defining moments of my life. It is also one of the events of my young life that I feel was a lucky opportunity. Being placed in the Children's Home was the event that saved me from what statistics show should have occurred. There were hard times growing up in the Children's Home, but compared to the daily beating I endured as a child, it was a sanctuary and a beginning for learning about faith and power of love. I know that it has helped to shape the person I have become.

When you feel that life is constantly beating you up, that every turn and step leads to heartbreak or hardships, it becomes hard to stay in a place of peace and happiness. Still, you must find the inner strength to stand up and take those steps that will lead you to a well-deserved and happy life. The difference between those who can tolerate the challenges and broken dreams and those who can't is like the difference between those who create a successful life and those who don't.

First, I would like to share with you a little background information about myself and my journey so far. It starts with hopefully creating a vision for you of how my childhood, which was very nontraditional, shaped me and my journey in life. It still impacts decisions and choices that I make today. It has shaped who I am, and continues to influence who I am still to become.

How many of you, during your life at one time or another feel like people are wrongly judging the "book cover of your life"? One of the most misunderstood things about life is the fact that most people's "cover on their book of life" or who they appear to be does not match the real person or journey they have been on. My life has been spent with people making judgments, based on first impressions, about who they think I am or where I came from. Most have completely misjudged me. However, over the years, I have become use to it, and even expect it. Most assume that I am a prissy girl who has come from a privileged life surround by opportunity and stability. It might surprise you to know that nothing could be farther from truth, except me being a bit prissy.

I was born to a woman who was still a child, and who was poor, uneducated, insecure, and very emotionally needy. I was born to a man who was still a boy, and who was also uneducated, mean, self-centered, and weak. My parents were children when my mother at the age of seventeen and my father at the age of sixteen became pregnant with my sister. I was the third child born in a family of seven children—all within an eight-year span. My brother and I were born exactly eleven months, three weeks, and two days apart. The time span between the others is almost the same. I last saw my mother at the age of seven; she left us alone, and I only saw her one time that I remember after that. This led us to being raised in a home with my father and stepmother. After my mother left, my father brought into our lives a woman who beat us daily for the next four years. Now you tell me how well do you think this story is going to turn out? Statistics say that it won't. I believe that you do, at some point in your life, have to make some very serious and major decisions about what you will allow in your life and what you will not. We all have hardships and disappointments, no one person has the market on bad things happening to them. Some people might think that I am being harsh when I say that most of us have designed our lives by our own actions and decisions, therefore we find ourselves on a path that we continue to destroy or create problems for ourselves, our families, and children. We have not yet learned the value in being honest with ourselves and others by admitting: "I created my mess."

When we learn to accept our role in our life, that is when you learn to develop personal integrity based on actions that only you know about. You need to answer to yourself whether you are being the best you can be, or not. I realize that there are those who have found themselves in a dark place by no actions of their own. Children, for example, can never be held responsible for the life they are born into. Though they must take responsibility for what they become, not falling into the trap of "it's because it's all I know" or "it's how I was raised." Being a victim with the mentality to blame others and not take accountability for your actions will never serve you well. A lot of people play this game for their entire life, affecting others with this lack of growth. They continue bringing chaos to the lives of those who are associated with them as well. That doesn't mean that they should not be given the chance to change and fix the problems. If people are willing to accept the personal responsibility and learn the tools to redesign their lives, then it is never too late. I also believe that more people would accept advice and help if they knew how to start and where to start. You cannot change when you have no knowledge of how to go about it.

That is my purpose for writing and sharing my story. I am hoping that the guidelines that I used in my own struggles and disappointments can help others to begin their journey for changing decisions and patterns in their lives to make better choices ... to take those steps in becoming who they always believed they could be. These are simple guidelines almost elementary in their approach, but simple is sometimes the best place to start on a new path and journey.

My older brother had become my protector very early in life. He would place me and my little brother in his small, twin-size bed near the wall to make sure that I was safe when our mother would have men spend the night in our home. Later, when we were in a foster home, he would again protect me. He was constantly making sure that I stayed near him. I was too young to understand, and he was too young to explain that it was a very serious and unsafe environment for me. It was a big responsibility for a young boy to make sure that his little sister stayed out of danger. Two of my sisters had the misfortune of being a part of the statistics of two out of four young girls being physical and sexually abused, and both were molested at a young age. Growing up in this unsafe environment, I was fortunate to have someone like my older brother. Without him, I am sure things would have turned out very differently for me.

After we went to live with my father and stepmother, my first lessons in forgiveness came from learning to forgive my father, who had brought us into the home of his young wife who beat us. The beatings began almost immediately, and they lasted for close to five years. This woman had dragged me across a room by my hair more times than I can count, beating me with a hairbrush. She was the woman who would pull me from a deep sleep in the middle of the night, throw me to the floor, and kick and hit me till I had the burning sensation all over my body from the slaps and kicks. After one of my brothers was accidentally dragged by the car as it was moving down the road, she then took him home and put him in a tub with Lysol of all things, never seeking medical treatment for him. We were so fearful of retaliation; we didn't dare say anything during the accident or while she placed him in the tub. I still have no understanding of how one human being could come to possess so much anger. One look from me or my siblings could cause uncontrollable outbursts from her.

We all had practiced keeping our heads down so that we would appear invisible to her. She truly must have had a cruel soul to be able to knock my baby sister out of her highchair and bust out her tiny teeth at the age of two. My older brother would try to explain away the marks on his face by making up stories about a cat we didn't have, when he was questioned at school about the bruises and fingernail scratches. The fear was overwhelming and the eruption of violence unpredictable.

I remember the summer I spent in bed when she pushed me down the stairs as I carried an arm full of rugs, she had stacked on my arms so high that I could not see over them. I was supposed to take this mountain of rugs down the stairs to shake and clean them. When I stood, my leg was totally turned and twisted in a wrong direction. She readjusted my knee by hand and put me to bed for weeks as it healed, never seeing a doctor. I can still remember the horrible sound of the cartilage of my knee as she twisted it back into place with her hands. I remember the horror and disbelief. I never said a word, not even cried out in pain for fear that she would do something even more violent.

There was this time when I broke my lunch box thermos by accident. She picked me up by my shirt and pants and decided she should throw me through the large glass window of our home in New Orleans. Thank God she didn't, but the fear was psychologically terrifying.

There are also the memories of being placed in the corner with my knees crossed and my head hanging forward. These punishments could last as long as eight hours during summer when school was not in session. She would walk by and kick me in the back and slap my head as I set in the corner helpless. These were especially scary times, because in many instances, we didn't know why we were being punished. I remember the fear I felt as she entered the room, not knowing when the kicking would begin. It was a mind torture, not knowing if she would do it this time. I would try and make myself as small as I could in hopes of being invisible. I and my siblings still talk about our times spent in the corner. It was a punishment we all endured. None of us were spared from being punished this way. My siblings and I share a learned sense of mental strength because of what we experienced.

We always revisit these stories when we have a family gathering. We do this, I believe, because we still find it impossible to imagine doing any of these things to our children. Also, I believe that it strengthens our bond, knowing that we have survived together. When I speak of the disappointment, I have for people who use their abusive childhood to justify their terrible actions toward their children or loved ones—this is why. It is unimaginable to me. I always say "You know how it feels, so how could you inflict such pain on those you are supposed to protect and love?

Because of these experiences, this is where I learned to pray. This is where I developed the faith in hoping, praying, and believing that we would be set free from this situation. I would pray that God would send a "good family" to take us away. I didn't know what that looked like, but I just knew by instinct that it was possible. With the innocence of a child, I believed with all my heart that it would happen.

Things changed again for us when my older sister decided to run away, hiding in the orange orchards near our home, refusing to tell the authorities who she was. In previous times when she had run away, she was returned to my stepmother and father, who would only beat her worse than before. The day my sister ran away for good, my father and stepmother packed us up and moved us to Fort Pierce, Florida, in the middle of the night.

None of us asked questions about where she was, because we were never allowed to speak to them without first being spoken too. Then we were allowed to answer only with a "yes sir or no sir." To speak to our parents was impossible because of fear. I had my first real conversation with my father when I was twenty-three years old. I had not seen him, except one time, for thirteen years. He had come to visit my grandparents, and I had a discussion with him about the abuse. He denied that any of it ever happened and told me that I was "remembering things wrong." He died without ever acknowledging his actions. I made a choice to let it go. It was never worth the argument to me. The truth could be backed up by my five siblings, and that was good enough for me. I guess you might say that I felt he wasn't worth the time or effort for me to convince him of something I knew to be the truth. I had little or no respect for him, and I knew that the time spent on it would be wasted. I only felt sadness for him as a human being. It was not hard for me to forgive such a broken soul.

The abuse continued for the five of us after my sister ran away. The only thing I knew was that my older sister never returned, and even though I had no idea where she was, I hoped it was better than the situation I was in.

Then came the day I refer to as our deliverance. My siblings and I returned home from school to find our home empty of our father, stepmother, and half-sister's personal belongings. My father and stepmother were nowhere to be found. Our father and stepmother had left with our half-sister.

The most powerful memory I have is about the five of us sitting on the screen porch, trying to make sense of what was happening. Abandoned again, but instead of the fear I felt the first time a parent skipped out, all I felt was relief. I find it amusing that this is how I really see this event in my life. It was a time of joy almost. I guess, as a child, your memories help to protect you, remembering only the nice ones. I remember it as a fun time. My brothers say that we would not eat for days and be so hungry. I truly do not remember the hunger. Most people, especially adults and parents, would be appalled at the horror of leaving five children under the age of twelve by themselves in a house, but I was just relieved to not have to worry about the beatings anymore. I look at that day as a blessing and answered prayer by God. For the first time in our lives, we were able to play like children.

We jumped off the roof of the house playing Dracula, mowed the yard to make a racetrack. We were our favorite race car drivers and ran a race around the track. We also played cowboys and Indians, always arguing over who would be the Chief and who would be the Indian. We would swing our younger sisters over the ditch beside the house, which was filled with water and copperhead snakes.

After a few days of running wild and carefree, we found a dime and decided to walk to a store, all five of us in a row, to call our grandparents in Nashville. My brother remembered their number. He has always had an excellent memory. We all walked to a store with a pay phone. My brother placed the dime in the payphone and dialed. The number went through, but a dime doesn't get you much time. As my grandmother answered, the connection was broken. He did not know about asking someone to accept the charges, so my brother never spoke our grandmother. The disappointment was devastating. It was a really pitiful sight to see five young children walking back down the highway with no hope—crying and scared to death. Yet, no one stopped to help us. When I think of us that day, it is still so clear in my memories that my eyes fill with tears for the pain and anguish we all felt.

I find it amusing that no adult stopped to check on us as we walked back home to the house crying. I am sure that if that situation would have happened today, someone would have stopped. Things were different then. People viewed abuse of children very differently. My grandparents were loving and wonderful people. Unfortunately, they were unable to monitor the situation since my father moved us around so much. They fought hard to keep us siblings together as a family.

At last count I believe it to be somewhere around fifteen different homes in which I had lived before the age of eleven. I honestly can't remember all of them. My brother drove my husband and me around one Friday after Christmas to show us some of the homes we had lived in Nashville before our move to Florida. We visited most of them, somewhere around ten. This was before I was eight years old.

When we returned to the little house to sit in the screened porch, it started to rain and thunder. I remember saying to my brothers and sisters that God was speaking to us and he would send help. Our father soon started to drop by with food and to "check on us." These visits would normally last less than an hour. Just long enough to remind us why we were glad he was gone. He would visit once a week or sometimes it would be longer—sometimes allowing our food supply to run very low or even out. It never occurred to us that this was not normal. All we knew was that our stepmother was gone and we were happy about that.

Years later I learned that he and my stepmother had moved about twenty minutes away with our stepsister. He would drive by late at night to see if we were inside the house. We usually weren't, choosing instead to stay outside in the dark and play. We often wondered if it was him driving by and would throw ourselves on the wet grass and lie very still as not to been seen until the car passed.

One day our father returned to take away my two little sisters. People from the state came soon after to get my two brothers and me. We were then placed in a foster home which had a lot of children. My memories of this time are almost nonexistent. Before the summer was up, my grandparents came to the foster home to get us and bring us back to Nashville. I later learned that they had been looking for us for almost a year. My grandfather went to the home of a judge and took Jack Daniels whiskey and cigars as he sat in the backyard and convinced this judge to help him find us. It took another year, but my two younger sisters were found, and we were reunited. Our family was back together—the six of us.

My grandparents took us back to Nashville and made a decision that was very difficult for them, but a decision I am grateful for. The church, which my aunt attended, told her of the religious based group children's home in Middle Tennessee. My grandparents could not afford to take care of us. My siblings and I would go to live at the Children's Home in the fall, September 17, 1969. When they told us of their decision, I ran away crying and thinking of the Shirley Temple movie "The Little Princess," where they think her father died and she is placed in the attic by the people at the school. I was sure my experience would be like that. But it wasn't, instead we were each housed separately in large dormitories by age and gender. I was on the third floor with the ten and eleven years old with a tiny bed/cot to sleep. I also would walk across campus to help make breakfast for over 100 children each morning at 5:30 before going to school. I feel sure that this had an impact on my work ethic that was developed very early.

It took years to convince our grandparents that they did the right thing by placing us in the Children's Home. Even up until my grandfather's death, he always felt guilty. He would ask us all the time to forgive him. I would always tell him that there was nothing to forgive him for. He and my grandmother made a decision that would give us the advantages we would never have had without growing up at the children's home. It was a blessing and a gift. I still look at my time at the Children's Home as the answer to my prayers as a young child. It might not have looked like what I had in mind, but I learned that God answers your prayers. I learned that lesson young. God has a very good sense of humor, it turns out. As a young kid sitting in the corner and praying for "a new family," my prayers were answered in a most unusual way.

My gratitude is to the people who worked at the Children's Home and gave of themselves and their lives to care and teach us faith, self-respect, and love. I also realize that I must be very honest about the fact that it was far from perfect or normal. It wasn't always great. One of the hardest things for me to overcome has been to realize that I am not betraying the Children's Home by talking about the hardships of growing up there. I still try to honor the place which I know helped to save my life, which I will forever be grateful for, and which I believe was still a better choice for most children who were there. The work they do with children is very importance and necessary. It is sometimes the only "safe" environment that a child can have.

These experiences that were challenging were also one of the reasons that I started college four weeks after graduating from high school. I knew I would age out of the Children's Home soon and had nowhere else to go. I enrolled at Belmont College. I remember being dropped off with a single box, a rocking chair, and a "good luck!"

It probably sounds strange that an eighteen-year-old would consider a rocking chair her number one possession. It was the last Christmas present that I requested from the Children's Home before leaving. It was a symbol of family to me. The one I didn't yet have but dreamed of. It was the dream of one day rocking a child that would belong to me. I protected and guarded that rocking chair over the years. With all the moving and hardships, it encountered, I made sure that chair was always with me. Today my daughter has it and will one day hopefully be rocking her babies in it.

No one from college knew until my second year that I did not have a home to return to. I would pack my things and move to the dorm that was opened to the kids who could not go home during the holidays, because they lived too far away. I stayed in the dorm during every winter break, summer break, and never returned back to the Children's Home. I also worked at a department store in Green Hills for extra money for personal items. My room and board were covered, but toiletries and clothing were not. Since the school cafeteria was closed on weekends, meals became another added expense.

At the age of twenty-two, I went out into the world, going into a marriage with the only boy I had ever dated. He was two years older than me and raised at the Children's Home since he was three years old. Looking back, it is not surprising how two young people raised in a group home could ever understand what a healthy relationship or marriage would look like. I remember as I walked down the aisle crying and being so anxious, because deep inside, through the intuition that God gives you, I knew that this was not a good situation. We divorced exactly two years to the date of our marriage when I discovered that he had been cheating the entire marriage. This challenge taught me to acquire the backbone and toughness that would carry me through the rest of my life. Before the divorced, I was a self-described doormat with a proponent attitude of making everyone else happy at my expense and all the bad decisions I made were connected to this attitude and lack of value in myself.

We had moved to Alabama for his job, and once we divorced, I moved back to Nashville with my car and my clothes on my back. I had nowhere to stay, no family that was able to take me in. I was fortunate that my college roommate's parents let me live with them until I could get on my feet. In exactly three months I had gotten a job, saved money, and moved into my own apartment. This began my journey of making very intentional decisions concerning the choices and actions I would make in my life. It started a discovery of my talents for being able to deal with people, and that left a positive impact on them.

I became one of the youngest Sales Mangers of the BBB, performing at a high level of success, to a Real Estate career of starting my own company, but not quite as successful, except with the life lessons I learned from the failure. I married again, about five years later, to a man who also became the father of my two children. We divorced about fifteen years later, again because of his infidelity. That season of my life was one of the scariest. I went through depression, despair, betrayal, and incredible pain. It, however, made me the woman I am today. It taught me about the place of despair that could be so deep that you would want to end your life. My pain was deep, strong, and unmanageable, so much so that I considered ending my life and those of my children.

Whether I was hallucinating or whether it was real, my grandparents who had both passed away appeared to me and told me to contact my sister at 2:00 a.m. I did, and she came and stayed with me until my personal doctor's office opened and we were waiting on his doorsteps. I had lost all hopes. It is still a bit frightening to know that any person is capable of thoughts of taking one's own life. Once I started to heal from the loss and pain of my divorce, I also started to become more independent, capable, and fearless in my direction for my life.

I returned to the Real Estate Industry and began to create a life and purpose I would be proud of. The person I worked for recognized my ability to work with people and asked me to build a new real estate-based business – The Appointment Desk. I utilized my experience and contacts to successfully build the call center as well as serving as the sales/operations director. This experience enabled me to have success in creating a name and brand for myself. The Appointment Desk experience helped me to earn the trust of our clients. That trust and my integrity enabled me to become known as a loyal and dependable person in the in the Real Estate industry, with opportunities beyond anything I could have ever dreamed of being possible.

God has placed three men who have given me protection and safety. The gratefulness I feel toward them has left me with an attitude as if all wrongs from my life as a child have been corrected. The place in my heart for forgiveness and acceptance is in part possible because of these three men. First is my brother, Jimmy, for a watchful eye and his protection over me as a young girl. Second is my boss, Jon, who gave me the opportunity of a lifetime. He believed in me until I started to believe in myself. His generosity, guidance, and mentorship put me in a position I had never dreamed was possible. He has been a man who has kept his word beyond what anyone else would have done, or in my opinion was even required. He has taught me so much about personal integrity and how doing the right thing is more about your honor than what people know or see. It is about a promise given and an act fulfilled. It has enabled me to have a financial success that is truly a gift. The third is my husband, Mike, for his unconditional love, support, and safety. He has given me a life any women would be thrilled to have. I feel blessed and lucky that he chose me. His ability to make sure that I feel loved and adored every day was what I prayed for in a partner.

I literality prayed for this man by name. I asked God to send the man he knew was perfect for me, what God knew I needed. I ask God as a sign that he had sent this man, that his name be Michael. It did not matter to me what he had or didn't have. I didn't make a long list of his personal appearance and attributes. God knew already that he had to be trustworthy, have honor, integrity—those things that a person would want. What God made sure I had that I didn't know I needed at the time was someone who was unselfish, funny, emotionally healthy, had understood boundaries, and was a gentleman, fun, and exciting. Most of all, God knew that I had never had anyone in my life that made me feel safe. I have felt safe since the day this man decided he wanted me as his person. There is no doubt in my mind that without these three honorable men of integrity, my life would have been much different. I thank God for them each and every day.

In 2012, I had a back surgery when my L3 started to crumble and parts of it became lodged in my nerves. For almost five weeks, I laid on my stomach, not moving, because the pain was so horrendous. I could barely walk, sit, or stand without the pain causing tears to run down my face. I was forced to slow down and reflect on my life. I made two major decisions concerning where I wanted my life to go and how I wanted it to look and feel.

The first decision was that I wanted desperately to find my purpose and my calling. The thing I had been created to do. Three years earlier, I had started the process of creating my motivational speaking program to assist people with finding their success and accomplishing their dreams. The "Stepping Stones" seminar program had been finished for over two years, yet I never moved forward, believing that I was not capable and no one would really want to hear it. My dear friends, who believed in me more than I believed in myself continued to encourage me almost daily. Like most people I had a lot of excuses. I had dozens of reasons why I would not be able to do it.

During this time of lying there in pain on my stomach before surgery, something took hold. It was a small voice that said to me, "If this was it and I never walked again without this tremulous amount of pain, would I be content with what I have accomplished with my life so far?" The answer to that question was a huge "no." I became determined and convicted that I would create my dream and purpose with no more excuses. This time I would try for something that had real value in my eyes. I would inspire people to follow their dreams by telling my story. Sometimes it still amazes me that once you set your mind on something, the opportunities and doors start to open. People start appearing in your life that become vehicles to getting started on your path of purpose. Once I made this decision, I found opportunities to take writing and copyright classes. I was able to do volunteer work for the Children's Home, doing fundraising, speaking, and mentoring. I got involved in other charities and groups. These opportunities started to present themselves to me at every turn, without me even looking for them. It was again proven to me that once you make some major decisions about your path and purpose, doors start opening as if to say, "You are on the right track." God's power of opening the door that will help you on your path will be presented to you. You must then have the courage to walk through those doors.

The second decision I made was to allow a partner in my life. To find someone to share my dreams, hopes, and desires with. I realized during my illness that I had been closed off in my personal life. For more than three years I had been afraid to allow someone to really share that part of me. I was not emotionally ready to take that step, and that I had put up barriers so that no one could get close enough to me. In part because my heart was not ready and also because where romance was involved, I had made a few bad choices about the type of men I had chosen to share my life with. The men I had chosen had been emotionally unavailable and felt comfortable to me. It has been hard for me to pick a partner when I was not sure what normal looks like. I did know now what I wanted it to feel like. In every relationship, I have always given more than I was given back. Again, this was a flaw in my personality of believing that everyone would treat me how they were treated.

I do not blame anyone but myself for my choices. Learning that men and women are different creatures, and that they should be treated as such was an important part of preparing myself to be a good partner. A man cannot give you everything, as you as a woman cannot give a man everything. I now know that I must give myself the most important things such as respect, worth, love, acceptance, and joy.

I started to work on becoming a better partner so that I could expect a better partner. I was lucky to find the love of my life. I received from him my most treasured gifts. The gifts that were most important to me. These gifts were of safety, being adored, admired, respected, and giving as much back to me as I gave to him. We liked each other as people and that is a hidden gem for a successful relationship. You have to have more than love; I feel you have to really like that person as well. I was blessed to become his wife five years after we met. I have finally found my safe place to breathe. We grew through the rough times and respected the journey that was not always easy or perfect. Our mutual respect and the pure joy for each other made our love strong. I now believe in happy ever after.

I will share with you the "Stepping Stones" that I feel can help to transform you, to make some lasting changes in your everyday life. It begins with a conscious choice of changing your approach to your circumstance and how you perceive them. Some of these choices I made at a very early age and others I made along the way with the process of life changing myself.

It is not always easy. I have been there. I have lived the thoughts of wanting to give up and crying out to God for His mercy, or, at the very least, His acknowledgement that He knew I was alive. I have felt lost, alone, and just plain forgotten. However, each time I was able to look deeper inside myself for the strength to find that hope, belief, and determination to lift my head and heart. I truly believe that there was purpose and reason for each and every one of my challenges—and that they were placed in my life as lessons to learn and grow.

I have given you the background information on some of the challenges I have had to face so that you will understand that I know how you feel, and I have been there in that place of darkness where you are not sure whether you will be able to pull yourself out of it. I want to share with you the steps I took to build my faith, strength, and ability each time to move forward and reestablish the belief that I needed to find joy in my life. I used five basic steps:

- Acceptance and Forgiveness is the Key
- Knowing Who You Are and What You Stand for
- Determination
- Goals: Choosing Your Path
- Faith and Hope

I hope to assist and motivate you in getting to a place where you can take a look at the choices you have made and reprogram your way of thinking that will start you on a journey that helps you get to your ultimate peace, joy, and happiness. Isn't that, after all, what each of us are searching for? We are all searching for that feeling of worth and purpose—our reason for being. I start with acceptance and forgiveness. Because I believe that all journeys really do start here.

Acceptance and Forgiveness is the Key

The first step in changing your circumstances is accepting your past. It can't be changed no matter who you are, but you can learn to cope with the challenges of your past and grow from them. The greatest battle will be fought in your mind. You must learn to accept where you came from and then find the strength to forgive the injustices that you have encountered in your life.

Sometimes we play these injustices over in our heads. We dwell on the bad things that have happened to us. We let them define us and allow them to keep us from becoming who we want to be. That is why it is important to practice cutting off those negative thoughts that fill up our heads.

When going through my divorce, I was introduced to a method of visualizing—a "stop sign." When my mind would race to those negative, destructive, and hurtful thoughts, and I began to panic, I was told to imagine a stop sign and say very loudly in my head, "STOP!" I needed to find a way to stop the thoughts which played over and over in my mind: "Why was I not good enough to hang on to a man I was good to? What had I done to make him have a yearlong affair right under my nose? Why was I so stupid that I didn't even see it? Was I too fat or not pretty enough?" These thoughts can paralyze you to a point that you become unable to function.

I was taught by a counselor how to train my mind to see a big red "Stop Sign" every time my thoughts started in that direction. Memories of the morning I walked in on my husband 's phone call with his mistress haunted me—I would go numb at the thought of his words to her, nausea would overwhelm me when I thought of the sixteen years I'd spent with him. Just two days before hearing that call it had been our fifteenth anniversary The feelings of betrayal and heartbreak were immediate. I had been clueless. The humiliation and betrayal I felt was all I could think of.

I often still wonder why when we feel that kind of pain and heartbreak, some go to a place where we blame ourselves and beat ourselves up because someone else didn't have the integrity to be who they should have been in a relationship. I had to use the "Stop Sign" trick so many times that I couldn't count. It was extraordinary how over time that process started to work and I could change my thoughts instantly. I still use the "Stop Sign" technique when I start heading down a negative path of thinking, and it can be a great tool for you as well.

The process of the divorce took over a year and a half to complete, with pain that brought so much fear and abandonment issues back to me from my childhood. The only thing I wanted was to feel safe and find some peace of mind. My two children were always at the forefront on my mind. How would I put their lives back together and help them to feel safe again? Divorce changes everyone. It changes how we think, how we feel, and who we then become. I wanted so desperately to feel whole again. I felt like I would never know happiness or joy. I knew that I had to focus on something else—anything except my fear and pain.

I decided to fight the battle in my mind, not to become a victim. I decided that I would start to change my internal dialogue to include the qualities about me that were good. I would work on the negative qualities I didn't like about myself; I would work to change them. Instead of telling myself that I wasn't educated enough, I started back to college. Being with young adults that were eighteen and nineteen years old was not exactly a breeding ground for building your self-esteem, or so it seemed at first. Being around young adults who would ask my opinion and advice did help to rebuild my self-esteem. Taking that first step was the beginning of building back my confidence.

To say that I was not technologically literate at the time would have been an understatement. I didn't even know how to turn on a computer. As I found myself ready to flee from a class that was all about power point, the instructor saw my panic and assured me that I could learn. I found that my teacher was more than willing to give me extra help and many of my fellow classmates were willing to teach me as well. And they did teach me—willingly and graciously. Angels really do exist in the unexpected help of others. We only have to open up and accept the opportunities from people whom God places in our life. We have to be vulnerable enough to be teachable and coachable.

I found myself a year later being hired to do marketing and public relations for a telecommunications company by accident. I told them that I was not good with computers and was told that they wanted me for the qualities I had. They wanted the qualities that no one could teach to anyone—the skills I had acquired by life's lessons and instinct. They wanted my people skills and likeability quality. They would be happy to teach me the rest. It turned out that my talent of relating to and making people feel comfortable was a marketable talent.

If I had not had the experience of being raised in the Tennessee Baptist Children's Home, I would not have developed the ability to feel compassion for and relate to almost all people who I meet. Growing up with over a hundred vulnerable kids made it easy for me to see who a person really was and how to connect with them. I have learned that most people will show you their best when they believe that you recognize that they have "a better version of themselves". They want you to understand them and their value.

That is a basic need for all of us. We want someone to accept us, without judgment, as we are.

Before we can find the value and acceptance in other people, we must first find our own value and acceptance. Again, you cannot change where you came from, who your family was, or any of the experiences that happened in the past. You can, however, deal with it. Accept that you are who you are and what happened to you has happened. I know it sounds simple, and it really is. We make things so hard. We try to find answers to situations for which sometimes there are just no answers. "Fair" is not a reality most of the time. When my children were young and would say, "That's not fair," I would always say to them, "You are right. It isn't and most of the time it won't be. Decide to move on in spite of it and make your own choices based on what you want. Don't wait on 'fair'—it probably won't come."

Here is the bad news about "fair"—it doesn't happen for most people, only a selected few. If life has been fair to you, praise God and be thankful, you are one of the lucky ones. But most of us have some sort of unfair past trauma. Some people have a "that's not fair" moment that is more damaging and horrifying than we can imagine. Still, each of us must make a conscious decision to accept our "that's not fair" and move on. The good news is that it's a choice you can make.

I truly believe, and it has been proven to me over and over, much to my horror, that someone else's bad situation can make yours look like a cake walk. I have met women who awe me with their strength. It has taught me that my situation is nothing in comparison. It is also why I didn't write my book for so long. I didn't understand why anyone would find me special or interesting or inspirational after what I heard from these ladies.

I learned through great encouragement from friends that all those "that's not fair" stories are important and can be the message that someone out there will need. So, accept your life experiences and make them count for you. Use them to find strength, inner strength that only you know you have. You can use where you came from to relate to and be of service to others. You can use your story and where you have been as lessons that will lead you to the best you can be. "That's not fair" happens to everyone. Be the one to make it count, not the one who lets it hold you down and destroys you.

I wish there was a magic bullet for forgiveness, but there isn't. Acceptance will start to lead you toward forgiveness. Accepting your past is a process of learning, gaining knowledge, and coming to a place of understanding for the people who have hurt you. I had to accept the fact that my parents were not equipped at being able to give to seven children the love or guidance that we needed. They simply did not know how. Let me say this is not an excuse for their actions, just a fact. No one can give to another person the things they do not understand or know.

What I do want you to understand about my parents is that I feel like they could have been less violent. They could have decided to take care of their children. Instead, they chose to put themselves first and continue the toxic patterns that were probably passed down to them. In turn they allowed innocent children to live in a destructive and violent atmosphere. Our father chose to put his desires and wants above us while allowing our stepmother to abuse us daily, and our biological mother chose to pretend that we never existed while living in the same city we did. She had made that choice to pretend until she remarried, moved to Florida, and even till she died that none of us were ever born—a decision supported by her parents, sisters, and that side of the family. All of them helping to protecting her so that her husband of over 40 years would never know we existed.

They had the opportunity to work through the victim mentality and let go of the past. They chose not to create a life that had personal integrity.

Finding people who will listen to you so that you can voice the pain and frustration of your past and even your present challenges is always helpful. Be careful about who you choose. Make sure that they are people who encourage your growth and not those who help you to make excuses.

After you've decided to accept your life as it is, then comes the really hard part. One of the most important things you must do to move on is learn to practice forgiveness. Most people I talk to say that it is the hardest thing to do, almost impossible. But I ask you, do you want peace? Do you want joy? Do you want to be able to function at some level of greatness or at least be able to say you can perform life as you imagine it? Then forgiveness is a major key. Without the ability to forgive, you really can't get to full acceptance.

I learned forgiveness early. I learned that God expected it, and as a child it was a simple lesson and more easily learned. It was a lesson that would serve me well over time.

We have all heard the saying that forgiveness is the key to happiness. Our first instinct is to resist and wonder why the people who have hurt us should be forgiven. Our inner voice screams at us that they do not deserve it. The pain they created does not justify a right to it. What I believe is this: forgiveness is not for them, but for you.

Forgiveness is for your sanity and how you look at the world around you. Bitterness is ugly and it is a cancer that stops all positive actions and thoughts. This is also where all journeys must start along with accepting the realities of your life. I tell you this because some would think that forgiveness should have been hard for me. In fact, it came easy as a child. It was only harder in my adult life to practice the art of forgiveness.

Forgiveness, is it easy? Not usually. I am grateful that I had the adults at the Children's Home who guided me and raised me in the church. They helped to make it easier for me to forgive. They helped to make it possible by having me around the church and the teachings of Christ. I have never struggled with forgiving my parents. I somehow knew that they were not equipped to be parents, and that they too were damaged, angry, and unhappy. When you can look at people without trying to mentally insert yourself, it can be easier to see the reason situations exists.

Years later, my stepmother called me when her daughter, my half-sister, was stationed in Iraq. My half-sister was near a reported bombing and this prompted my stepmother to call me. For the first time she admitted that she was frightened that God would take her daughter to punish her for the abuse she did to us. I started to cry immediately. Not only because she was finally acknowledging what she had done to us but also because she was so afraid, and I had never seen that side of her. I told her that I would pray with her that her daughter, my half-sister, whom I did not know, would be safe. I told her that the God I knew did not work that way. That he was not a God of pain but one of protection. I also remember being so afraid and sorry for her. I was a mother of two very young children who were my life, and I couldn't imagine the pain of losing a child. This was the day that completely gave me the closure and forgiveness toward her that I needed. I saw her two times years later. She just looked broken, old, and sad.

Forgiveness is a gift you give to yourself. The Bible says that you cannot be forgiven unless you forgive. What I do know, because I have seen more than my share of people who are bitter, is that holding a grudge is not pretty. It does not allow you peace, and it will never allow you to find true happiness or joy. The accomplishments in your life will never be fully enjoyed with hate in your heart. I know how hard it is. It was easier for me to forgive parents who brought pain and fear, but much harder and a bigger battle to forgive my ex-husband after our divorce. I struggled for years, and when I thought I was doing well, something would cause the bitterness and anger to build again. It has taken me years to forgive him and the woman that he had the affair with. I can say with certainty that I have finally found the grace to forgive and wish them only good things. My son and daughter built a relationship with their father they had sought to have since they were very small children. My ex-husband has become someone who they can count on and feel loved by. It is truly a gift that came from such sadness and pain. I am happy to say that I can look at him without bitterness, pain, or being hurt. We are able to spend time together as a family. I also want to take this opportunity to express my gratitude for the financial support he gave to me and my children during our divorce. I am truly grateful and know that it made our lives much better because of him doing the honorable thing in financially supporting his children and me.

I will share with you one of the best techniques I was taught by a brilliant man whom I have been blessed to have in my life. He shared a way to practice forgiveness that changed my life and how I viewed praying for forgiveness on behalf of myself and others. He said to pray for 28 days for the person you want to forgive. Not the prayer that most of us pray including me, which is "Lord help me to forgive this person who wronged me." Instead, it is a prayer that requires a powerful leap of faith. He said to pray, "Lord I pray for favor, for good health, and for exceptional things," on whatever person you feel has offended you. It is hard the first few days because it goes against our nature. By the second week, I was starting to feel the changes in my spirit and in the very being of my soul. With time, I found that it transformed who I was. He gave me a gift that I will treasure and will always be grateful for. He gave me the wisdom and power to change something in my life that I now know was one of the reasons he was placed in my life.

You, too, can start to come from a place of love and acceptance in all of your dealings with people. It has made my spirit rise to a new level. A level where negative treatment does not have the same effect as before. I can become totally detached more easily without judgment and hard feelings. I have realized that I do not have to react. That is power. Power that can change you with a strength that you never knew you had inside of you. Finding and giving forgiveness is the key. Is it easy? No, but I am saying that it has to be done or you will never reach the potential that was intended for you.

Do not allow anyone the power to adversely affect your behavior. I have always felt that when we hold anger and bitterness in our hearts and thoughts, we are giving power over to someone who should never have it. Why you would give so much power and influence to someone who intended to cause you harm? Take back your power and be in control of your emotions and how you choose to react to wrongs done against you. Forgiveness and acceptance can set you free. The first stepping stone of changing who you are meant to be is accepting and forgiving.

Suggested activities:

- Write a letter forgiving those who have wronged you.
- Write a letter asking for forgiveness from those you have wronged.
- Write a letter of forgiveness to yourself.

Knowing Who You Are and What You Stand For

I have always heard it said that "If you don't stand for something, that you will fall for anything." Knowing who you are and what you will accept from people in life and what you will not accept is so important. It determines the types of decisions you make and how they affect your life. I made some very serious decisions about what I would allow in my life and what I wouldn't very early. I always shared with my children when they were older how important it was to never let anyone lead you down a path you not want to go. I was always strong enough not to place myself in situations where I would end up in an environment that I did not want to be in. I realized later in life that it was because of a healthy fear of knowing I had no safety net. If I allowed myself to be led to a decision that would be harmful or place me in danger, there would be no one to turn to or call upon to help me.

One of the major decisions I made was that I would neither as an adult give someone the power over me nor place myself in a situation in which I would be abused. I made that decision when I was eighteen. That was an incredibly tough year. It was the year when all my friends from high school and I were getting ready to attend the prom and graduate. As pictures were taken for the prom, there was really no one there to make a big fuss over me. My girlfriend's parents were taking pictures, hiring limos, and having parties. I just put on my yellow dress, yes yellow, without much fuss or celebration. My sweet grandparents had bought me a prom dress from K-Mart. I chose a yellow granny type of dress with a lace up front. Later in life when I showed the picture to friends, they laughed and remarked that all I needed to go with the dress was a pair of some combat boots to make the look complete. Well, my good taste for fashion and dressing with my own unique style was something that I acquired later in life.

Between the facts that I knew I would have to leave the Children's Home when I was graduating soon and had no family to return to. It was very scary and painful. At high school graduation, as all the other kids had their families around them, I felt really lost. I became angry over my circumstances for the first time. It was a time when I had changed from the little girl who sang in front of church groups almost every week and stood in the spotlight, to being quiet, pouting, and withdrawn. During that time, I was confused, causing a negative attitude in place of my normal upbeat, happy and quite content outlook. I now recognize it as fear.

I realize now that the people who were in charge of me, my upbringing, and my mental health, were ill equipped. I found it incredibly hard to voice the feelings that were so overwhelming. I don't remember anyone even asking me about those feelings or concerns. The situation was very much like my arrival at the Children's Home years ago. No one once ask a question about my life or treatment before I arrived. As a child you do not think of those things as being necessary to be asked by adults who are responsible for your care and upbringing. So, it never occurs to you that it might have been helpful to a child if someone knew their past and the trauma they had been through. It was only later, when as an educated adult and having children of my own, that I realized that it would have been a helpful tool in not only assessing a child's mental and emotional state but also in repairing some of the damage caused by their past.

I know that the majority of the reason for the lack of questions was due to how things worked in those days. It was a time when you raised a child in a church with good values, hard work, and structure, and they would turn out okay. In the 60s and 70s psychiatry was for the rich, not for the everyday person or child. I still believe that most of this is a good thing, but knowing what we know now about psychology and the importance of helping a young child would have been such an advantage for so many children being raised at the Children's Home. As I look back today, the progress I have made really becomes evident by sharing my story. I realize that for more years than I care to say, I never even once looked at my past. As a teenager not once did, we at the Children's Home talk about where we had come from or the abuse and neglect we had lived through.

What is amazing is that it never seemed abnormal. It certainly was not something that was financially available to the children at the Children's Home. The Children's Home was funded by the donations and generosity of the local churches and people in the community. The Children's Home was also not connected to the Social Services of Tennessee in any way, because it was a private organization. There were no counselors on site that I remember. I would assume this was the reason no one asked me about my life before arriving at the Children's Home or what I had witnessed or lived through. This was how I learned that you don't talk about bad things. I never saw a reason for years to do so. It is fascinating that I first started speaking of it when I was almost 50 years old.

You handle your problems or challenges by pretending that it never happened and move forward with your life. It is of no surprise to me now how difficult it must have been for a lot of the children during that time who lived at the Children's Home. It also explained why so many were angry and violent as well as did not have much success with their futures. Don't think for a minute that I blame the Children's Home or feel somehow let down by this discovery. I understand how those "times" were and how things were done during that period. What they did give us was as much of a safe environment as they could, love, respect, and a spiritual foundation. For some of us, that was enough. The strength that we had to overcome all the abuse, neglect, and other horrible acts against us is something that should be looked at as a badge of success in spite of the fact. It certainly looked like no child could or would have success after the life they had been dealing with. I am proud to say that my brothers, sisters, and I, who were raised at the Children's Home, did succeed when it certainly looked like we should not have. We beat the statistics against the odds of a positive outcome. We never should have, according to the experts. I think this goes to show that people, children especially, can overcome any thing if they are given the tools to learn. I also feel that this is where personal integrity comes in. When you do the right things, the hard things, and the work of growing and learning, then there will be successes in your life. Demanding more of yourself than other people would demand of you. You must first be responsible for your own actions and decisions and be accountable to yourself.

When I started on my journey of writing this book, I literally cried for over two years. It was the first time I had allowed myself to look at my childhood and young adulthood and acknowledged the trauma I had lived through. It wasn't always great, but I had to be ready and able to look at the truth of my childhood, instead of blocking out and ignoring the fact that nothing was normal or, most of the time, wonderful about it. I have only been able to do this in the last ten years. My way of coping before that time was sheer gut control of feeling that reliving it would never serve a purpose for me or allow me to succeed. It became even harder once I started doing fund raising and speaking on behalf of the Children's Home to overlook the challenges that must have been difficult during the 70s. Today the Children's Home is more equipped to handle the children of trauma who end up there. The people who care for these children are also trained and better equipped to help these special kids through the challenges and struggles that they face daily.

The hardest part for me has been to realize that I am not betraying them. I still honor a place that I know has helped to save my life. It is a place that I will forever be grateful for and believe that it is still a better choice for most children, who have been raised there. The work they do with children is very important and necessary. It is sometimes the only "safe" environment that a child will have.

I have had to overcome so many events that included being fear based. It is the most powerful emotion I carried with me through my lifetime and one I had to move into unwillingly. I never questioned the adults about the decision they made. Authority of any kind was not something I ever questioned. I believe now that it was because of the deep memories and fears I had for authority figures of any kind. Also, there was that part of me that took what was dished out to me and made the best of it. That is where my strength and power came from. Although I have passed on a few opportunities in my life, because of fear, I am proud of the fact that I have also walked through many obstacles even in the face of fear. Learning to balance fear is a hard one indeed. It can either take you places beyond your imagination or can stop you dead in your tracks. Conquering fear is a challenge to be practiced and learning to understand the power behind it.

The house parents that I had when I was moved to a new cottage away from my family in my senior year did not have the best intentions for me, I believe. They were cold, aloof, and certainly not what I needed at such a fearful time in my life. I don't recall any encouragement from them. I remember this was how I first learned from adults about how "prissy" they thought I was. When they did talk to me, it was more from a place of accusing rather than comfort. I did not fit the narrative of a child who had been abused and carried a chip on their shoulder. I always felt that they resented the fact that I truly intended to do better with my life than what society expected a child from "the Children's Home" to believe possible. I know now that they were probably just frustrated because they were ill equipped to really handle the emotional problems that we as children from abuse and neglect had. I also later realized that those house parents, as a young couple with two young children of their own, were going through some personal issues of their own. I did not trust them and could not explain all the fears and emotions I had.

Talking about your deep dark fears is not something anyone wants to share with someone they do not trust.

I was taken from the comfort of living with my siblings, because the adults in charge of me made a determination of what they thought was best for all of us, and moved me to a new cottage with new house parents. I am still shocked by their lack of knowledge of the pain that was caused to me. I was an easy child to deal with. I am also amazed by the person I had not yet become, who went willingly so as not to seem ungrateful and cause any problems—the good girl who did what she was told and still smiled through it all. I thank God for the growth and backbone I acquired over the years.

One day after being moved to the new cottage, the housemother verbally and physically attacked my friend Virginia, who lived in that same cottage. Virginia was the first to befriend me when I came to the Children's Home, at the age of eleven. We had absolutely nothing in common through the years; she was the risk taker, boy crazy, and a wild child. I was a speaker for the Children's Home, the soloist for the Children choir that traveled to churches almost every Sunday, and the girl who got the Citizenship award almost every year. She was a rule breaker and I was the rule follower. I still have the same mentality or feeling that it is very important to follow the rules. So, I married a guy who does not follow all the rules, only the very important ones, so that he can bring a little excitement into my life. Virginia made me laugh, and I still have fondness for my friends who live a life a little out on the edge, something I was never comfortable with but find joy in watching from afar.

Virginia and our housemother had a huge fight one night that also became physical, and I never trusted that houseparent again. I was shocked at the anger and fear that rose up in me that night; memories came flashing back so strong. It changed how I felt about these people who were supposed to be taking care of me at a very challenging and difficult time of my life. The housemother reminded me so much of my stepmother with the same look and hardness on her face. I withdrew and became more of a loner.

Virginia was taken away and I didn't see her again for a very long time. It was years later when she was married and had a young son of her own that we reconnected.

This experience was also one of the reasons that I started college 4 weeks after graduating from high school. I enrolled in the summer semester and continued to live on the campus throughout the May semesters, fall, and winter, choosing to stay there during the holidays, except for my first Christmas at Belmont. I had returned to the Children's Home for a few days, feeling very out of place and sad.

It was my second year of college before anyone discovered that I was staying on campus all year long. One day a friend of mine asked me about my Christmas and what gifts I had received. I then explained to her that I stayed on campus, because I did not have a place to go. I told her that I was raised at the Children's Home. She was shocked because I was always so happy and seemed so content. I still remember how all the girls in the dorm wanted to hear about my life and started to share my story with other people at school. The story was always "it was great" and very little about my childhood before going to the Children's Home. It seems strange to me today when I finally look at that time during my life and my reaction to it. I would tell people that my parents had left and didn't want us. It was how I handled things and I am grateful for what I feel is a part of my personality—a gift I was given by God. It was the strength He gave me to not look at the downside of things, but to be hopeful and grateful for the good around me. I believe it also had to do with the fact that when you do not know what normal looks like, it is easier to accept the abnormal. Again, children are resilient in almost any situation.

From these experiences, it also helped me to develop my decision to never let anyone lay a hand on me violently. I believe it made a difference in the direction my life could have taken. It helped that I was a loner in a lot of ways, not being connected to any one group of people. I could and did fit in with almost any group of people—not totally on the inside of any group, but always on the fringes of each group of relationships. Later in life, when my children were just babies, I had my first experience of letting people into my life and making lifelong friends, instead of being the girl whom everyone liked but no one really knew. The women I met while my children were in preschool and elementary school became a new experience in friendship for me. I allowed them to really get to know me and I stepped into their world. Some became the family that I felt I never really had. I am proud to say that I still am friends with most of them.

Often, I have wondered at the choices I made and how, in some ways, they kept me safe from the drug scene, sexual premises, abuse, and other events that could have led me down a path of destruction. I realize that I was the exception to the rule coming from my background. I truly was on my own. The dream for a life that I had visualized was more important than any instant qualification of any kind. I later realized that my strict discipline of being a rule follower served me well as a teenager and young adult. I was conscious of the fact that I never had a safety net. There was no one to call or ask for help if I got into trouble. I realized that one small infraction could be a disaster to me.

I am happy to say that I feel my brothers and sister also made some very good choices about what they would accept and allow in their lives as well. One thing I am very proud of is that each of us in regard to our children made a decision that we would raise them in a loving, caring, and nonviolent home. We all accomplished this. That is a miracle in itself not to have passed on the cycle and pattern of behavior of violence.

There is no doubt that we each loved and raised our children in a supportive and safe environment. This was a decision, a choice, a line drawn in the sand. There would never have been another choice other than this one for me. I am proud to say that my siblings and I, coming from a horrible childhood, were able to break a terrible cycle of violence, within our generation. This is what success looks like. Both from the influence of the adults from the Children's Home and our own choices to be the best we could for ourselves and our children.

That is what I mean about knowing what you will and will not accept out of people and life. It has to be conscious, and it has to have the power and determination behind it. It has to be the decision where you say, "No more, not ever again." You have to decide that this is where you will stand in the face of fear and hardship; this is where you must make a stand. I feel sure that there is always that moment in time for each and every one of us. I have found that most face it and come out on the other end better because of knowing what you will accept and not accept in life. Some people however refuse to make those hard decisions. Not making these decisions keeps you on the same path with no change, no hope and the belief that there is no way out of your current situation.

It can be done. You can change your circumstance, and therefore you can change the outcome of your life and what you pass on to your children. It also must be done. The outcome is based on the integrity of the choices. The choice of putting someone else's needs and safety above your own wants and desires is important. Blame is pointless. It does not let you advance in life, ever. Life experiences that seem unfair are sometimes just that, unfair. I considered it as simple as "someone had to pull the short straw" and that just might have been you!

Doing the work of challenging yourself beyond those limitations is the journey that will define whether you will be successful in life or not. Real integrity comes from decisions made when no one else is looking. It is when you demand more from yourself from a higher level than others demand from you.

Taking pride in knowing yourself is a very powerful and important way to personally measure how you will decide to live your life. I truly believe that is why there are some people who walk this earth, and you feel the difference in them. You can't quite put your finger on it, but you know they are different, they are special, and they have something that the rest of us don't have. It's that they require or demand more from themselves than an average person. They demand the highest level of integrity from themselves.

This is a level above average or normal. My ex-husband's grandfather, Father Frederick Isacksen, had this "thing". One could feel it when you were in his presence. He was a minister who had an energy that was love, kindness, and compassion. He was truly a man of God. Your level and standard of integrity you demand from yourself should always be higher than the standard anyone else will put upon you. Then the question of your integrity is something you, without a doubt, are confident in.

However, we fudge in areas of our lives, because no one else sees or it won't be found out. We are safe from the public eye and can pretend to be more honest than we really are. That is when we compromise our integrity right off the bat. We expect less and perform from that standard or concept, thinking no one will know but me. We hedge and push the real quality of "who we are" further back. If you truly are determined with becoming the "best you," and living your life with the utmost integrity, then this evaluation should cause an uncomfortable feeling in you. You should be most concerned with the judgment of your actions that you do not share or show to others. You should look at your opinion about your integrity, courage, and compassion as honesty as you can. If you will follow this guide of living with personal integrity, putting the importance on your hidden personal integrity, those actions that others do not see, then your public integrity will not be questioned. I challenge you to expect more from yourself.

Where do you go from here and who you are now? Who are you really? What do you stand for? How do people see you? How do you see yourself? Your choice, your decision, your actions—they all define who you are. You have to care enough about yourself and even more about someone else to make these hard choices. You have to decide whether you want to be a person who is self-centered or a person who puts the welfare of others ahead of yourself. You have to decide if the people in your life such as your family and your children are going to be more important. These decisions will always bring with it a crossroad of choice. How you choose decides your future. It also can decide the future of your children. Especially if those desires are the ones that will put you or the people you love in harm's way.

Those wrong turns can place you in a situation that looks hopeless. What do you do, and how do you change your life? It starts with creating a vision or a dream of what you want your life to look like. Write it down. Do not trust your memory; it is easier for you to see what your dreams look like when you write them down. You remember them, and by looking at them daily the desire and belief becomes more powerful. It is like a road map for you and your direction. You can't get where you want to be, unless you know where you are going. Once you know where you want to go and who you are, then amazing things start to happen. God starts placing people in your life that have the same interest and vision as you, and these people become the positive, encouraging helping hand that you need.

When deciding on who you are or who you want to become and what you believe, you will sometimes have to leave people behind who have been in your life. If someone pollutes your life with negative thoughts and actions, you must remove them or at least limit the time you spend with them. This is not easy, I know. This is another part of living your life with integrity. It is a choice that almost everyone who has ever changed their life has to make. Sometimes they are family members and close friends. If you can't remove yourself completely, then you must limit the access they have to you and your mindset. Surrounding yourself with like-minded people is important. A person who is positive and who wants the best for you is also important. If you don't have those people in your life, find them. They can be found in the church, in a lady's group, a men's group, and even in a business group of successful people.

I have found that truly successful people do not mind mentoring others. True success always comes with the help of someone who made the time and taught what they know to someone else. These people are everywhere. You do not have to find them. They will find you. All you have to do is be open to allowing them in. Open to trusting them and accepting their friendship, guidance, and the knowledge that they can introduce to you. You have to be coachable, trainable, and, at certain times, fearless.

It is not an easy process. Your own doubts will again, as always, be your own worst enemies. But each step you take that leads to a small victory will make you stronger and give you confidence. You will grow braver and stronger when you see that you don't die, the sky doesn't fall in and you don't go up in a puff of smoke. The worst-case scenarios do not happen. Then courage sets in, confidence sets in, and finally the belief in you sets in.

I have been lucky to have such people appear in my life. After my divorce, when I returned to work again, after being a stay-at-home mom, people were placed in my life to help me. I did a lot of volunteer work during my "stay-at-home" time, which I am now so grateful for. I worked as the Chairperson for fundraiser on at least five different projects during that time. This kept me out in the business world and little did I know that I was really building my skills at sales and public relations. I later learned that even though I sometimes worked up to 40 hours a week doing these fundraisers, without pay, the experience was priceless when I had to reenter the work force. I had developed some major skills that lead me to a career in sales, marketing, and public relations.

When you know yourself, you have to also make a plan for change. Sometimes making a plan teaches you more about yourself than anything else. This is a hard process, because here is where our insecurity starts rearing its ugly head and tries to knock us off course. This is where the self-doubt comes in, the times when you start to second guess yourself and become your own worst enemy. As I write this passage, I am so struck by the doubt that is still inside of me and rearing its ugly head. You see, I wanted to share my story for years. For years, it has been a "plan" of mine. For years, it has been a calling that is deep inside of me. And for years, I have struggled with the little voice that says, "Who are you to think that anyone would want to hear from you? What makes you so special? What have you got to say that would help anyone?"

That is when I thank God for the people who I have surrounded myself with, these strong and knowledgeable friends who believe in me. These are true friends in my life who have been encouraging to me and my dreams. They are my support system. They were the ones who pushed me gently and not so gently at times. That is why surrounding yourself with friends who are your biggest champions is so important. They hold you up when you are unable to stand up on your own. Find these people and add them to your life. They are out there, and once you have the intentions to change your life, they will show up. When you are looking for an understanding of your purpose, a quiet voice, in my case I believe to be God, will tug at your soul. It becomes harder every day to ignore that voice. Then the challenge becomes how and when you decide to step out and start the process.

You must take steps to put your plan into action. Writing down your plan is always a good idea. It is okay if your plans change along the way, just rewrite the plan and make the adjustments. During my time of taking personal development seminars one of the exercises was usually a mental one of "Go back to your dreams as a child, try to remember what you wanted to be." I would get so irritated by this process. Although I know it is a good one for most people. It is remembering your dreams as a child, what you wanted to be, how you saw yourself, and what you wanted the most to do when you grew up. Whenever I was in this situation of looking at my dreams as a child, I would start to become very emotional and even angry. I realized that I didn't remember dreaming of what I would be, I was dreaming of getting out of the terrible environment of abuse and pain. I was praying for that "good family" to show up. My memories were waiting for the next beating or listening to my sibling being beaten. Who had time to dream? A good friend of mine, Robin, had a conversion with me when I explained to her how upset this exercise made me and how unequipped I felt. She said, "You are lucky because as an adult you can now build your dream with the knowledge and experiences of life that we as children didn't have. You will not be held back by the things you didn't understand or know."

Again, thank God for this amazing friend who had my back and helped me to look at my circumstances in a different and unique way. I could recreate my own dream and plan for my life from a place of knowledge. The sky was the limit if I only had the vision and courage to dream it.

I can't stress to you how important this step is in creating a new life. This is the process of knowing yourself. Knowing who you are, knowing what you believe in, and knowing what it is that you want your life to look like. You must be patient with yourself and the different processes of each experience that you go through. You have to take a serious look at the problems that you have in your surroundings, the people you associate with, and the patterns that lead you to where you are at this moment. Some of these experiences were by chance and came from no doing of your own. They were because of people who had a responsibility for you and blew it, people who did not have your best interest at heart or who had, for selfish reasons of their own, placed you in situations that brought harm and pain to you.

At some point, however, we have to all say, "Enough! I cannot blame who I will become tomorrow because of the influences and people in my life from yesterday." Take small steps to change anything that will change the outcome. Patterns such as hanging out with negative people and thoughts and attitudes of" I am not good enough". You must change your mindset to saying things like, "I am important," "I matter," and "I am able to change my surroundings and life with action." Again, if this cannot be done on your own, find a set of friends who will encourage your new journey. With their encouragement and support, you will be able to make the changes you seek.

Work on yourself daily by reading some books that will give you knowledge about life and relationships. There are numerous books on communication and skill development. There are countless books and authors that all share the same knowledge of changing your surroundings and your mindset. Write down affirmations about things you want in your life and read them daily. You must place positive messages in your life each day. These messages should be of hope and the possibility that great things are available to you.

Again, I am not saying that it is easy. I have had struggles with being insecure and hopeless many times, even when I practiced and read daily. The way I handle these times of insecurities is to make sure that I read more encouraging words and that I pray a prayer of gratitude. It is hard to be fearful and hopeless when you are truly looking at the things around you that you are grateful for. My list every morning always starts with my children. I am grateful they are safe and amazing human beings. I am grateful for my friends who are there for me with words and actions of support or a shoulder to cry on. I am grateful that I am healthy. I am grateful that I have a job I love. I am grateful that I have a car that works well. I am grateful that I have a home. I am grateful that I am able to buy grocery. If you can't think of anything to be grateful for then start with, "I am grateful that I am breathing." I admire the people who do not have the basic needs and can still stay in a place of gratitude.

We have all seen or heard of these warriors, angels on earth who can smile and laugh along their journey with amazing fortitude. Their suffering, which they seem to hardly notice, is God's messages to us all. They were chosen to share their faith and stories to teach us about being humble and grateful as we continue the journey of our own lives.

In making some very serious decisions in my life, decisions such as, I will not accept being in a violent relationship, also that I would walk through the fear of the unknown even if I shake from that fear; the decision I made to always put the children I brought into this world first and protect and help shape the people they would become through positive love, actions, and example. I know that is what helped to shape me into one of the lucky ones, one of the ones who defied the odds, who broke the pattern of abuse, and who passed on to a new generation of healthy life skills and possibility of becoming whom they dreamed they could be.

There are other accomplishments that I have made, but I mention the ones that relate to my children first and foremost. I do this because it truly is my best work, my best decisions and choices when I was at those crossroads of choosing how my life would look. They are my best contribution to my life, to their life, and to society. I am blessed to have had the motivation of these two beauties in my life. My true family started with their births?

Another good way to start this journey of discovery is to write down defining moments in your life. These are the moments and experiences that made you who you are now. Even the bad experiences can contribute something beautiful and powerful to your life. It all has to do with the way you look at them. This is where that step of accepting comes in and where you say to yourself, "It happened, and it is my truth." Find the power in the fact that you survived it. That is the real power—power that can help you to accept and move on by using the feeling and pain to say, "No more, I will rise above this and find a way to use it as a tool for growth." If you are unable to do anything else, you should recognize the greatness in yourself for making it through that challenge. Be proud and give yourself credit for the inner strength you might not have ever looked at or examined before. It truly is an accomplishment.

Let go and embrace those experiences as a measure of how far you have come. Use them to measure how far you still need to go to become who you were designed to become. Then set guidelines and boundaries concerning the people who you allow in your inner circle. I mention this again, because allowing the wrong people into your inner circle is usually the downfall of your growth. You have to be strong enough in yourself and your journey of healing to let go of the comfort of what you are familiar with. Familiarly is always the easiest, but most of the time, it is not the best thing for you. Allowing a group of people or one person who has been constantly in your life is good, but only if they bring value. If these people do not bring value or worth to you, then let them go. People have stayed in the same destructive place because they could not remove themselves from dangerous situations, because they need to feel and see familiar situations and familiar environments. They mental and physically go to what they know.

The great thing about improving your surroundings is that you can recreate yourself by the company you keep. It does take a re-creation of who you are in order to grow and change. Do not fear people who try to make you feel inferior. You will know them by the way they make you feel about yourself. I believe and have always believed that there are more caring and loving people in this world than people who are not so kind and generous. People most often will offer you their kindness if you expect it. By the same token, the people who are unkind, harmful, and judgmental will treat you this way in almost every situation you have with them. Remove them from your life or limit your time with them.

So as simple as it sounds, and again, you don't have to make things so hard, they usually aren't, to find out who you are. Spend time with yourself getting to know yourself and deciding what you will accept and not accept from others. This becomes easier when you start the process of discovering who you are. Draw that line in the sand of what treatment is acceptable to you and what treatment isn't. It doesn't look the same for everyone. You recognize it by the way it makes you feel about yourself. Does it make you feel good about you? Does it empower you? Does it make you feel safe and able to be yourself? Does it make you want to move forward and grow? Ask these questions about the people in your life and then make the choices of continuing to have them as a part of your circle or not.

I hope you see and understand why knowing who you are and what you will accept is so important in the choices you make. We would all be so much better off if we knew who we were. Life becomes so much more exciting and enjoyable when we can discover that knowledge. It is still a process for everyone. It is a process that continues throughout life as we change and our circumstances change. By knowing who you are, you will be better equipped to make better decisions concerning your life. But the best thing is that you will make fewer mistakes that can impact your life in a negative way.

So, step into your new life by having the courage to let people know who you are. Do not let anyone lead you to a place where you do not want to go. Know what you stand for. Draw the lines in the sand of things you will accept and not accept.

Suggested activities: List 10 defining moments in your life. Be honest about which ones you could have prevented and which you could not have prevented. There is always a pattern in each person's life. Some choose to blame others, never acknowledging the choices they have made.

Determination

A s I start this section of the book, I still have the doubts that continue to show up. The fact that I am not a gifted writer tells me that I will not be able to do a great job. I realize that it is not always an easy process to push ahead and do something that is uncomfortable or that you feel for which you do not have the required skill set. However, that is where determination comes in. There will come a point in your life when you will be uncomfortable and will have to continue to push forward.

When bad things in life keep coming at you and it seems that they continually search you out, it is hard to stay focused and keep your belief that your dream is obtainable. This can be especially hard when you feel you have lived a life of doing the right thing, but you still see that there are people who take advantage of others, cheat at every opportunity, and yet appear to suffer no consequences. Seeing this, you can become discouraged. It can make you angry and make you want to give up.

Many people might not expect it, but I would say that the scariest and darkest period in my life occurred not during my abusive childhood, but well into late 40s and after my divorce. During this time in my life, things were changing quickly. My daughter moved away to South Carolina to attend college. I had broken off an engagement after an eight-year relationship, and also found myself without a job. The company that I had built and managed and had become my identity was sold. Although I continued my employment for the new owner, I hated it. The job and position I held that had become my identity, was gone.

This period was a very difficult time, and most people had no idea of the despair I felt and the thoughts which went through my mind. I found myself thinking, "If this is it, I am through with the struggle." I had lost my purpose. I felt I had lost everything. I felt defeated and had to do a lot of positive self-talk to get myself out that mindset. Once more, I dug deep within myself and refused to give up. Later I found that light, that little flicker of hope. I concentrated on that little flicker till it became bigger and I had my confidence and my belief back those things would be okay. I had to start completely over in an industry that had taken a big blow during the recession of 2008—the mortgage business. Help again came from God in a form of an unlikely angel. I had no idea what opportunities would come from this young man that would change my life in ways I never dreamed possible.

Jon and I met when we were each running different companies in the same industry. When the company I had built was sold, I went to work for the new owners. Jon saw that I hated working for this company and asked me to come to work with him.

Jon believed in me. I started to work for him, and nine days later, his company lost an important investor and had to shut down. Many people told me that they were sorry and that we were both out of a job. However, Jon is not a normal person, he is a man of utmost integrity. Jon came up with a plan to get us back in business, paying me out of his own pocket until we could get off the ground. He believed in me more than I believed in myself at the time. I jumped in and started to help him build his company and found my stride and my confidence once again. Together we became successful and built a successful mortgage team in the middle Tennessee area.

Jon made promises to me that he has kept, beyond what I know most people would have never done. He gave me a successful financial safety net. True integrity is a treasure that I have witnessed where he is concerned. If you are fortunate, you will have people placed in your life who will share this gift with you. Remember that you also have to have a life of personal integrity to attract these types of people into your life.

What I know now is that this period of my life was meant to be. Without those three events, I wouldn't have found myself where I am today. If I had not been determined in spite of my fear, my world would no doubt have looked very different. The life I had for over six years was familiar, but that doesn't mean it was the life I was meant to live. My ex-fiancé was not the man I was supposed to be married to and share my life with. I realized over time that I could not see myself creating a life with him. This was not because he was a bad man, but because my dreams and purpose would not have been possible if I had married him. My gut knew this, and my head and heart had to adjust to the fact, a fact that was not easy to accept. I learned to accept that Stevie, my daughter, was supposed to go grow up and start her own journey. I also decided to start a new position by quitting my job and accepting a new one. I realized that I had greater things in store for me.

It was time to learn new lessons, face new challenges, and experience new successes. All of which would bring me personal growth and teach me to let go of fear and come at life from a place of excitement and belief in my own abilities. Looking back, I now realize that those challenges were just that, challenges.

The challenges have to become just challenges and not overwhelming problems or despair. That is why it is important to have the right mindset. I wake up every morning and the first thing I do as I open my eyes is say my affirmations. I talked about how important this is in the previous chapter. I feel the need to bring it up the importance of mindset again because it is important while you are trying to find the determination to move forward. Then I ask God for favor and protection over a list of my friends, family, and loved one. At last, I ask for God's protection and favor on all that I do that day. It is hard for things to start off bad when you start off with a heart filled with gratefulness and thankfulness. Then that flicker of hope rises in you and amazing things happen that day.

As I practice being grateful and look at the people who continue to give so much to this world even in spite of the horrible situations they have faced, the determination takes over sometimes in the form of shame. At times I became ashamed of how weak I let my thoughts become and realized that I was practicing self-pity. Being the proud person that I am, changes mindset very quickly. You must find your "pulling up your bootstraps" moment or your "keep on going" moment. What it is that makes you feel strong and worthy again and restores the hope and possibility that you can accomplish your dreams?

I realized only a few years back the advantage I had over most people, while growing up at the Children's Home. When I talk about being determined and creating who you really want to be, I am fortunate to have had an exceptional experience growing up that enabled me to be surrounded by a lot of different personalities. This allowed me later in life to start recognizing the personalities and behavior of people once I had spent a small amount of time with them. This ability continued to grow quickly for me as I too matured and learned "who I was." I had grown up in an environment where I was able to see the destructive behavior of people daily.

I saw and lived among people who could not control their emotions, their anger, and their need to lash out. It was all around me constantly. Even though I wasn't always sure of how I wanted my life to look like, I always knew exactly how I did not want it to look like. Sometimes that is enough to make you strive harder to make sure that you do not behave and react in the way that you saw as destructive behavior around you. I just knew it felt bad, it was ugly, and it never led to anything good.

I have never known a time when temper and violence used in any situation had an outcome that was healthy or productive for the people who used them? Families who fight among themselves with these destructive family dynamics normally pass along this lack of control. Teaching the others involved in their lives this technique, they continue an unhealthy environment. These actions of destruction come from hurt, resentments, and not feeling validated or valued in a relationship. It continues to fester and become a person's norm.

However, you can stop it. You can change your family dynamics and the future of your children. It is not easy. Most successes in life are not easy. That is why not everyone is successful in their life. Most people are never willing to put in the time and change it takes to create a healthy environment. I know this is because it is human nature to always go back to easy and familiar. Also, when you choose this path to stay where you are, you are miserable. Just like everything else in life, it is your choice again. You get to decide what your life should look like. There must be no blaming of others, just you taking charge of your life. It is, after all, your choices, your decisions, and the consequences those choices bring that will always determine how you create the life you live.

Determination has got to be in your soul. It has to be planted deep within the dark places in which you want to shine the light. When you feel hopeless, you have got to dig even deeper to gain the strength of "battling your mind" instead of it convincing you to give up. Again, the "battle" will always be fought in your mind and you will win or lose depending on your determination and your mindset.

Find your strengths and weaknesses and make yourself accountable for changing your thoughts and actions. Put on the smile even when you don't feel like it. Surround yourself with strong, happy people, even when you don't feel like it. Read or listen to words of encouragement, things that will lift your spirit. Read about other people's journeys and how they overcame the hard times. When you can acknowledge the fact that most people have a worse situation than yours, and still, they have the strength to continue, it can be a transformative moment. There is always someone worse off than you. I now recognize that I was lucky enough to not be the type of person who dwelled on negative and difficult challenges. It is also important to be determined to make promises to yourself.

Personal integrity is that you keep the promises you make. It's the things nobody else knows exist. You have to care enough about yourself and the outcome of your life to make decisions that will improve you mentally, physically, emotionally, and spiritually. This means setting boundaries with people who are not beneficial in your life's journey of being the best you can be. Personal integrity is making a plan and being determined not to let others get you off your path.

Determination is getting back up over and over again. Determination is not stopping to feel sorry for yourself. Determination believes that you can achieve your dreams, even when things don't go as planned. Get up, rearrange, redirect, redo, and keep going. Determination has to be created through the promises you make to yourself, through your personal integrity, through what you do when no one is looking. Your dreams have to become bigger and more desirable than your reality.

Suggested activities: List 10 amazing qualities about you. Find ways to make them stronger through reading, practice, or classes. List 10 weaknesses which have held you back. Find ways to make changes in these weaknesses. Write paragraphs on how your strengths might overcome your weaknesses.

Goals: Choosing Your Path

S etting goals is a way to measure where you have been and where you are going. If you do not make a conscious effort to design a plan, it is hard to accomplish your dreams and desires. Goals are a measure of how much farther you have to go to get where you want to be.

Where are you going? Where do you want to go? What are you trying to do, and how does that look in your mind? By setting goals, you can take baby steps to climb toward your vision. The small steps should be honored and recognized as the accomplishments that they are. A pat on the back for a job well done is important in continually moving toward the finale destination. The really amazing thing about self-development is that you can continually grow and change with each goal you reach. The desire to obtain more knowledge and improve your abilities grows with each goal that you set and reach.

The first step in setting goals is to decide what it is that you want out of life. This is why it is important to know your dreams and desires. Sometimes these are buried deep inside of you. Some people find it difficult to go to that place because of insecurities or a lack of self-esteem. A helpful exercise is to write down some of the weaknesses you feel you have. Those can be things about yourself that you feel make your goals or dreams unobtainable. The next step is to number them in the order of easiest to change to the hardest. Then take little steps to start changing these weaknesses to strengths. Do you need more education? Some of the education can be done through reading books and online information. The library is a free source to you, use it. Are there qualities about yourself that you could change without anything more than practicing simple disciplines? Examples of such simple disciplines can be, following through, being on time, and being someone who does what they say they will do. Do you need to have better control of your emotions or your reactions to your emotions? This is a quality that holds a lot of people back from success. Work on how you react to adversity. Are you a procrastinator? Work on setting deadlines and making sure you reach them. These are just a few of the shortcomings of most people. This is the part of being honest with yourself about who you truly are. You cannot deny about your character and hope to make important changes to your life.

Also write down the qualities that you have that you feel will make you successful at your goals and dreams. Are you good with people? People skills can be translated into income very easily. The better your people skills become, the more value you bring to the table. Are you trainable and coachable? Are you willing to learn? Do you take accountability for your actions? Asking all these questions may take you out of your comfort zone. Whenever you are setting new standards for yourself, it will always feel uncomfortable. That is one of the ways you know you are challenging yourself and your abilities. To be successful, you have to deal with the truth. You cannot change something if you are not honest about it. By being honest about what you want and what it will take to get it enables you to move on to the next step, which is setting realistic goals.

Setting realistic goals that are obtainable is a vital part of goal setting. They cannot be so big, overwhelming, or unreachable that you lose hope and faith in your abilities to reach them. This is what happens to most people. They make a huge map of their lives. Good intentions no doubt, but then they find it harder and harder to find some success or improvement and give up on their dreams. No one likes to fail, especially with the map they drew for themselves. You have to take baby steps that help you to gain the confidence. When setting your goals, make sure that they are obtainable—not so outrageous and outside of your skill set that you are hindered by your own ambition, but big enough that you will feel proud and excited about your path. However, they must be hard enough to encourage growth.

I like to write my goals first as ideas. I write them as affirmations. It is easier for me to visualize my dreams and break down the goal step by step. However, I am very careful about how much I put down at one time so as to not become overwhelmed.

Lastly, for any of your goals to matter, you have to take action. It doesn't matter how brilliant your plans are, if you never put them into action, you will never accomplish your goals. You have to move forward, even when you are afraid.

Many times, when I have accepted a new position, it has been in a field with which I had no previous experience. The people who hired me knew that I didn't have the experience, but either I convinced them or I was fortunate enough that they convinced me that I could learn the job anyway. Each time, I have held my head up high, projected confidence, and believed in myself. I would pretend to know what I was doing until I learned to do it. I had to put in the time to study and learn, but I can attest that this is a solid strategy for success. I have been fearless on the outside and scared to death on the inside. I have always been more afraid of failing at life than I was at a certain task or opportunity given to me.

However, you can and might fail at some point in your life. Being confident and "faking it until you make it" might not be good enough. It does not make you a failure at life, but it just makes you someone who hopefully learned some lessons of value to use later.

At the age of twenty-five, I met another woman who was in real estate. She convinced me that I could be a great real estate agent. The next week I enrolled in school, did my two weekends of classes, took the test, and was a licensed real estate agent within a month. I left my job at the BBB and started working for a real estate company selling condominium conversions, at the height of the negative cash flow age and sold them like hot cakes. Two older women with whom I had worked decided to start their own company and asked me to be a partner. It seemed like a good idea at the time. I remember I was fearless. This was a big mistake on the surface. I will say first of all I learned never go into business with people you don't know or into a situation you have not fully vetted. Never sign your name to pay back the money you don't have.

Long story short, as I worked hard to bring in money, my partners soon lost interest and failed to carry their weight. One of the partners disappeared with the furniture in the middle of the night. We held on for a year until we finally folded. I must say that this is the time when I appreciated my very new and young husband who was supportive, kind, and understanding. He believed in me even though I knew it was a very hard time. I paid back the bank with the help of a father-in-law who had been appreciative and proud of my entrepreneurship. My father-in-law was a man whom I looked up to and respected. He was someone whose approval meant a great deal to me. I walked away with a few lessons that I have never forgotten from this experience. I learned how to open a company, or perhaps how not to, and never to go into business with someone you have just met. It was indeed a failure on paper, but it taught me never to pass on an opportunity that could give me knowledge and new skills once I had weighed the cost against the loss or gain of the actions. I never saw myself as a failure, and again I was surrounded by people who encouraged and believed in me. My family let me know how great and capable they thought I was and how very proud they were of me. That in itself was worth the adventure to me. The price of trying turned out to be priceless. Do not be afraid of failure.

When trying to achieve your goals, it can be helpful to surround yourself with people who are supportive and give positive reinforcement. Positive feedback is so important. As I mentioned in the other steps for change, who you allow in your inner circle can make a difference in the outcome of your journey. It cannot be said enough, surround yourself with people who see value in you. Find people who are willing to mentor and help you reach your goals. The world is full of these kinds of people. God has a way of putting these people in your life, if you stop to recognize them.

I have found that most successful people share their knowledge freely. They are born leaders who understand that leadership is not being the boss, but finding the best in those around them and developing their talents. A true leader will understand the value that everyone can bring to the table. Seek out these types of mentors. Never underestimate God's hand in placing people in your life to help you achieve your purpose. I have been fortunate to have God place the most amazing people in my life along the way. I have realized that with the right belief in your goals and the right plan, God puts people in your life to help you reach these goals and dreams.

I believe that you need to surround yourself with the people who inspire you, the ones who you want to be like. If you surround yourself with negative people who play the victim and have no desire to better themselves, then you will be dragged down by them.

It is important that you challenge yourself. Figure out what you want. Take inventory of your strengths and weaknesses. Set some attainable goals. Put those plans in action. Do not lose faith in yourself if or when you stumble. Just. Set. The. Goals!

Suggested activities: Write a goal for each section: Physiology, Emotionally, Spiritually, Financially, and Relationships. (This is your Mission Statement of your Life)

Faith and Hope

F aith is the ability to hope for and believe in things unseen or unproven. Hope is faith in action. Faith is based on the hope that what you want is possible and will happen even without the knowledge of being able to see any physical proof of the same. Faith and hope give you the power to continue. Once a person loses hope, they lose everything. I often think of the people who made a final act because of a temporary problem. It is always a loss of faith and hope.

People do this when they feel there is no hope left. People also stay in their current circumstance because they have lost faith in their abilities. They lose sight of the flicker of hope. That tiny light in the distance is so important to keep your eye on. To believe that there is a chance, you have to believe in the hope and faith that things change and improve.

Once, I was asked a question by a gentleman when I attended a professional event that stopped me in my tracks. He asked, "Why is it that you continue to do cold calls and contact people who have already refused you? What is it in you that you continue to grow and change expecting a better outcome? You, who came from the background you did, while a person who was born with stability, support, and opportunity gives up the first time they are rejected?" He went on to explain to me saying, "When you will know the answer to that question, then you will know something important about yourself. It will also be your story to share to encourage others." I thought about that comment for days. Was it fear of failure or was it hope that maybe today would be the day that I got the sale? I finally realized once I spoke it—it was that flicker of hope, that belief in that tiny light of hope of the possibility that those things could work out. If I gave up today, would tomorrow be the day when they may say yes? I would not be able to do my work if I didn't practice a strong faith that things will work out for me if I keep one foot in front of the other. I would not be able to take the constant rejection that I encounter otherwise. I had to decide somewhere along the way to be a survivor.

I am lucky that in my young life I had already been challenged to develop my faith. This was why, after being abused and abandoned, I continue to believe in the goodness of people. This was why, after a divorce, I still believed deep down that "my person" was out there. I believed that God had a purpose and a plan for me to assist others, despite my own insecurities. I have naturally had faith in God's plan for me, even in life's worst moments. My faith helped to make me a good salesperson.

I have never been afraid of anyone else's religious beliefs and feel strongly that all people have a right to choose their faith. It is not my job to judge or decide what is right or wrong when it comes to questions about God. However, I personally believe it is so very important for people to believe in something greater than themselves. Call it God, the universe, or whatever else you wish. I know that not everyone will agree with this statement. I am okay with that. I firmly believe that when you directly tell people that they are wrong in their religious beliefs, you will never gain their trust or respect. If you wish to have a positive impact on people, you must first listen and respect them. I have always believed and still do that people are better judged by their daily actions than their words or religious identity. I practice the religion of Christianity and believe that Jesus Christ is my Savior. I make no excuses or apologies for it. That is my choice of religion, and I believe it to my core. I hope that through the love I give to people as they spend time with me that they will see the value in learning about the Savior I know. I have always decided to share my love of Christ through my actions. I believe, it is one of the greatest gifts God has given me—the gift of making people feel valued, cared for, and worthy. I recognize my job as a Christian is to love and care for one another as God commanded.

There has to be a light of hope, faith, the ability to believe that all things are possible with actions and positive thoughts. I personally believe that the power of prayer is my greatest tool in developing my faith. By practicing faith through prayer, I have become stronger. I do believe that faith in action can create new beginnings and changes. I still have the same faith as I did as a little girl sitting in the corner, not knowing when my stepmother would start kicking or hitting me, as I prayed for that "good family" with the faith of a child believing that God answers prayers. That is still an important and strong skill set for me. It keeps me going in the challenges and opportunities I encounter each and every day. My spirit is at peace as an adult with the belief of faith so strong that was cultivated from the spark of hope as a child.

Faith can be made stronger with practice. Practice faith every day. Every morning, you should know what your vision is and repeat it to yourself. Reinforce it by speaking it and seeing it in your mind. Find motivational thoughts and scriptures that will give you the foundation for believing that all things are possible. Affirmation is power if you do the labor, but it the work that goes along with your dreams. If no work is done, then an affirmation is just a delusion.

Make an affirmation statement about the things that are important in your life. Make statement about your occupation, your friendships, family, financial goals, and your mental, physical, and emotional health. These are statements about how things already look in your life and how they will look when you complete the work on yourself. Have the faith to do the work and believe that it is possible.

Turn to people in your circle who have faith as you do. They can be friends who will assist you in strengthening your faith as you go through the rough times in life. Find friends who will pray with you and for you. Become a prayer warrior yourself by studying what the Bible says about prayer and the practice of it. When your belief is weak, let others be the ones to hold you up as you grow from their belief and knowledge. I am lucky enough to have a very knowledgeable and strong prayer warrior in my group. Her guidance has helped to strengthen me and my friends as she would lead us each month in a power of prayer. My dear friend and "sister of choice" Lisa has been a constant source of knowledge, comfort, and a head of reason for me. She is truly a gift that God sent into my life. God will do the same for you. He will bring the right people to assist you in your growth and later send you to those who will learn from you.

Every now in then I hear someone say something to the effect of "if you do not expect anything from anyone, you will never be disappointed." That makes me sad to think that anyone can think that is a quality way to live their life. Disappointments are a part of life. I cannot imagine living my life expecting people, life, and circumstance to always bring disappointment. I have always and will continue to believe that most people are good and will bring value to your life. I have faith that good will prevail and that impossible just might be possible. I have one question. If you try and it doesn't happen, have you really lost? I say try. What have you got to lose? You have everything to gain. Give yourself the gift of not being afraid to hope and dream. Do not be afraid to have faith in something unseen. Do not be afraid to believe in the goodness of others. Will there be people who will disappoint you along the way? Of course, that will happen. It is your job to better prepare yourself for being able to recognize the honesty and goodness of people. Again, hope in action is faith.

Suggested activities: Write an affirmation for your life. Read a daily devotion to increase your knowledge and strengthen your faith. Daily write the things you know you are blessed with and the things you desire.

Final Thoughts

Today I have shared with you some ideas and thoughts that have been helpful for me and have empowered me. By continuing to do the work that we have started here today, you will be able to change your life and your path if you are willing to dream big and do the work and the labor that is involved. The hardest part will be letting go and learning new habits—habits that will set your path on that of change, a change in your life. Start small, get some successes under your belt and continue to grow and expect more out of yourself.

Accept the past and move on by having the courage to find a new path. Stop the old destructive ways. Practice having a forgiving heart and being slow to anger.

Know what it is that you want, and be willing to ask for help. If you don't know what you want, then you can't move to a higher quality of life. Be strong enough to draw a line in the sand, and have the courage to walk into your dreams and walk away from the habits of destruction.

Be determined that you will make it come hell or high water as they say. Be determined that you will pick yourself up off your knees each and every time, that you will not be a quitter, a loser at the game of life, and that you will not spend the rest of your life regretting the things you wish you had done. When trying to fulfill your dreams, hardships and problems weigh on you, but regret will kill you emotionally, never to recover.

Set the goals so that you have a path to travel on your journey, you have to know where you are going to get there. Then measure your progress. Make adjustments along the way if you veer off your course. A slight move or thought can make the difference in whether you will achieve your dreams and vision or not.

Practice faith every day. Every morning you should know what your vision and your dreams are and repeat them to yourself. Reinforce them by speaking them, seeing them in your mind. Find motivational thoughts and scriptures that will give you the foundation for believing that all things are possible. Affirmations are very powerful if you do the work along with the vision. If the physical work is not done, then an affirmation is just a dream.

Good luck in recreating a joyous and productive new life—a life that lets go of past hurts. Your cycle of loss for those you care for can be changed by you. Your future generations will benefit from the work you do to create a life you have dreamed of. Be accountable for your own personal integrity and growth.

Dedication

I wish to dedicate this book to the three most important men in my life. Each of them had a hand in changing my life for the better and made a difference in the outcome of my life. First to my brother, Jimmy. You have protected me for as long as I can remember. You were always the one to whom I knew I could run at any time. Your honesty, honor, and integrity have helped to keep my belief in the goodness of people. You were my earliest example of what a real man was supposed to be.

Second, is my boss, mentor and friend, Jon Sidwell. You offered and allowed me to have a financial life beyond anything I could have dreamed was possible. Thank you for keeping your words and promises to me. You are a man beyond the words of integrity and honor. You have always made it easy and a pleasure to speak on your behalf as we created our business together. It would have never worked with anyone else. I respect you, admire you, and am grateful to you beyond words. You are a and have been an angel sent by God in my eyes.

Finally, I want to dedicate the book to is Mike Ladd, my husband. You are my best friend and my soulmate. It is because of you that I now understand what soulmate means. You have given me everything I never knew I needed and the one gift I always desired—safety. For the first time in my life, I feel truly safe and adored. I thank God for you every day. You made the impossible possible. Because of you I believe in "happily ever after." You are my guy.

I would like to acknowledge a few girlfriends for their support and belief in my message; Terri, DeAnne, Donna, Christie, Bernice, Robin, Kim, Lisa, Cynthia, Laura. You lifted me up when my insecurities set in and my belief in myself needed a boost. Thank you to my two children, Tyler and Stevie for being great kids. I hope I make you proud.